bringing home Baby
from birth to 4 months

**Parent-Tested Tips for New Moms and Dads
by Jeanne Murphy**

SOURCEBOOKS, INC.
NAPERVILLE, ILLINOIS

Published by Sourcebooks, Inc.
P.O. Box 4410, Naperville, Illinois 60567-4410
(630) 961-3900
FAX: (630) 961-2168
www.sourcebooks.com

Originally published in 2000 by Perseus Books.

Library of Congress Cataloging-in-Publication Data

Murphy, Jeanne, 1964-
    Bringing Home Baby / Jeanne Murphy.
        p. cm.
    Rev. ed. of: Jeanne Murphy's baby tips for new moms, first 4 months. c1998.
    Includes bibliographical references and index.
    ISBN 1-4022-0539-2 (alk. paper)
    1. Infants. 2. Infants--Care. 3. Infants--Development. 4. Parent and infant. I. Title: Baby's first four months. II. Murphy, Jeann
1964- Baby tips for new moms, first 4 months. III. Title.

HQ774.M89 2005
649'.122--dc22

                                                            2005016463

Printed and bound in the United States of America
IN 10 9 8 7 6 5 4 3 2 1

This book is dedicated to my mother,
Bel-Mehr Mahar: a woman who was fortunate
enough to be completely natural with children
of all ages and stages, and someone who never
held back on giving me a simple tip to make
my life as a new parent easier.

I love you, Mom.

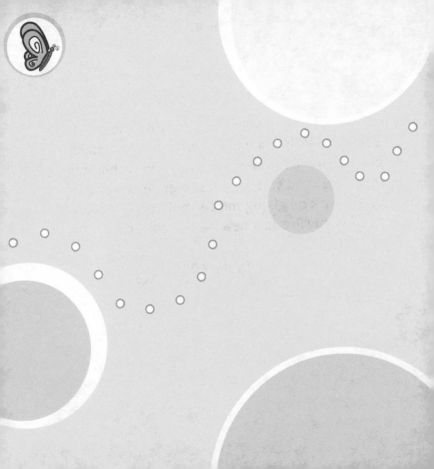

Contents

Introduction

Congratulations on your new baby. What a joyful time! And it can be a nervous time, too, as you learn all the new skills of parenting—and without much sleep! Remember that infants most of all need your love. There are lots of ways to be a great parent. I have collected all the tips in this book to help you through these first few months of learning about and caring for your newborn.

God bless you and enjoy every moment—it really does go by way too fast!

—Jeanne

Chapter One

Quick Notes for Working Parents

If you are employed by a company and receiving benefits during your pregnancy, spend time learning about those you are entitled to. The packages vary greatly, but they are your benefits and that's what they are there for. For example, your job should be there for you when you return as long as you give notification to your employer and follow their policies, so make certain you document *everything*. This will give you more time to relax and enjoy the baby with less stress and work on your mind. Even emails are usually acceptable proof that you've communicated to your work appropriately.

Take action steps ahead of time so you can savor your leave. For example, put an auto-reply message on your email that tells people you are on leave until such-and-such a date and not to expect a response from you. Give them contact information for the person handling your responsibilities and know that you've done what you're expected to do and even more by handling these easy issues on the front end.

Also change your voicemail and/or answering machine message at work to say that you are not collecting *any* messages, personal or not. And then stick to it! It's tempting to try to keep up with your work even if you're on leave, but don't even think of doing it. Not only are you going to want and need the time, you don't need to set that standard for others in your office. When a baby arrives, it's family time.

The proper way to handle gifts from your office is to send a thank-you note. You do not have to call unless you want to. The same is true for returning calls to your office and to anyone else for that matter. If you put a message on your home voicemail that says you are not available, that should send the message loud and clear. Get caller ID so you can decide which calls you want to take and let technology handle the rest for you. (p.s. In this way, we're lucky we live in this day and age.)

And remember, your new job is the baby!

3

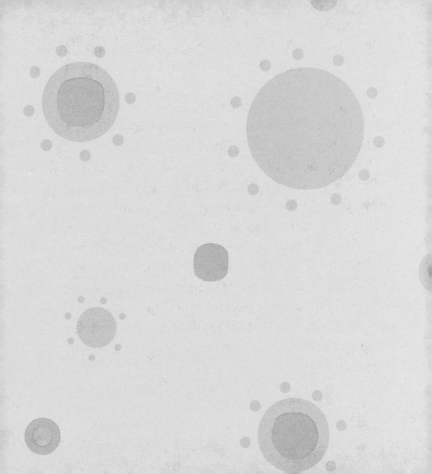

Chapter Two

Just Between You and Me

Communication is always the key to success. There's a philosophy that I follow that says, "If you don't hear anything from me, then I'm fine...*or* I'm up to something." This is generally true with babies. There's also a saying, "The squeaky wheel gets the oil." And that's what I think of when my baby is crying. After all, this is how he communicates something to me. But the truth is that really your baby is always communicating with you—either silently or loudly. Notice the little things, like whenever I noticed my baby dancing his feet, I knew that he was happy and I didn't dare change a single thing.

This book is filled with the most tried and true tips of parenting. If you read it once and find any tip useful, you might want to read it over and over again throughout your baby's first months.

In this day and age, courtesy toward and respect for other people's feelings, privacy, and their family is few and far between. Defend, guard, and protect your family at all costs.

Do yourself a favor and listen to the voice of experience whenever you can, whether it's from your parents, your mother- or father-in-law, another parent, or grandparents. Their hard work can save you a lot of time and energy.

7

The truth of the matter is that if you're happy, your baby will probably be happy too. That doesn't mean she isn't going to cry, because that's what babies do. And if you're not happy, your baby may not be so happy either. This includes your attitude and how fulfilled you are in life on many issues, like working versus not working, breast-feeding versus bottle-feeding, etc. You have to learn what works for you, your spouse, and your new family as you go. Try to be flexible in the beginning because it's a lot to take on at once.

$\mathcal{I}$n short, if you are an uptight parent, you will probably have an uptight baby, so take ten deep breaths when you feel this way. Remember to smile at your baby every time you look at him. This will change the mood for both of you.

$\mathcal{F}$orgive yourself if you make a mistake or lose your patience.

Don't worry, mom—it takes nine months to put on the pounds, so give yourself at least nine months to take them off. Drink lots of water and you're on your way.

The price for baby-sitters varies on where you live. To save money, your best bet is to arrange some type of baby-sitting that allows you to split up the time while you're out, especially if it's a long evening. Try using a baby-sitter for a couple of hours and then have a family member or friend take over from there.

Here's another great thought about splitting up the baby-sitting, especially in the beginning when everyone wants to see and meet your baby. Bring the baby with you to a gathering, then hire a driving baby-sitter or family member whom you completely trust to bring your precious child home. This way, you get a little time alone with your partner and everyone gets a little time with the baby.

As a parent, you need to learn to give up some control and even train yourself to believe in fate. This way, you will allow yourself to let others help you. Otherwise, you could overwork yourself and it will do damage to the entire family.

11

Options for care for your infant outside of the home when returning to work include: a child-care facility, a relative or friend, or another parent. I say if you want your baby to stay at your home, then you should probably go with a nanny. Otherwise, feel great going with a child-care facility early. Your baby will love it and the routine—and so will you.

Be aware that even when your family is standing by and/or volunteering to help with baby-sitting openly, it may become too taxing on them after awhile. The tip of the day, on days like this, is to be sure to pop in and take over again earlier than usual.

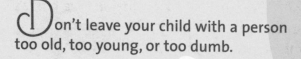

Don't leave your child with a person too old, too young, or too dumb.

To make it easier on you when leaving your child for the first time, visit the center or person's home often in advance so your baby is familiar with the environment. It's also smart to leave your child's special belonging— a blanket, toy, etc., at least for the first few days. Whenever you're leaving, try to keep in mind, "out of sight, out of mind" where baby is concerned. Some child-care providers say, "Short good-byes make for shorter cries."

$\mathcal{H}$ugs are one of the best things in life! Hug your new baby and tell him you love him as often as you can, especially if he is crying. Remember, your baby is trying to reach out to you and communicate without knowing how to talk. In fact, make it a habit to hug each member of your family everyday. Tell them you love them and how important they are to you.

$\mathcal{P}$eople used to tell me as a new mom that it gets harder, rather than easier. I think it's hard as a new parent because it's such a steep learning curve and because you can be so tired. But I believe once you get used to putting yourself behind your baby's needs, it gets easier...*much easier!*

$\mathcal{F}$rom the very first day, children keep their own schedules. They do some things the same way and time every day—such as bowel movements. Watch for the schedule and you will learn to relax. And if you help keep your child on her schedule, she will be more content.

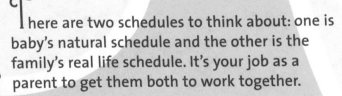

$\mathcal{T}$here are two schedules to think about: one is baby's natural schedule and the other is the family's real life schedule. It's your job as a parent to get them both to work together.

To learn your child's natural schedule, log his activities in a notebook or a personal computer over a twenty-four-hour period. Add information to your notebook every day. Fill in details, such as when he is alert, and even quiet but not sleeping. Post the schedule on your refrigerator and give your baby-sitter a copy because seeing it in writing will help everyone who's caring for the baby and especially *you*.

Consider the expression "adjustment period" to mean the time baby needs to get accustomed to your family's schedule, not the time your family needs to adjust to her natural schedule.

16

Leaving a baby in a car, running or not, locked or unlocked, is not only dangerous for the baby, but is also considered abuse and may be reported to the authorities, so don't do it, ever—not even "just for a minute."

Use a portable changing pad whenever you're visiting someone else's home. This could be one of the reasons for changes in friendships, which happens often after a baby arrives, especially if the friend is not a parent.

$\mathcal{B}$abies get cranky from overstimulation and so do new parents!

$\mathcal{I}$'ve always believed that infants know who they are when they look into the mirror by the way they look at themselves. What do you think?

18

$\mathcal{J}$f your baby rubs her eyes or moves her head back and forth, she's probably trying to say, "No, not this activity. Let's try something else and I'll be fine. If I'm not, give me a nap please."

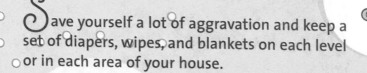

$\mathcal{S}$ave yourself a lot of aggravation and keep a set of diapers, wipes, and blankets on each level or in each area of your house.

When traveling with your baby, be sure to give the flight attendants advance notice if you'd like anything warmed. Surprisingly, they may have to boil water for you in order to warm what you need. Who would have thought that your travel plans could include these types of delays? Be prepared.

Baby powder will calm down and cool off your baby and you. Use it everywhere and remember it's also great for getting sand off your body, so bring along a bottle whenever you go to the beach.

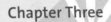

Chapter Three

Common Concerns

This is a true story. One day I went to the doctor's office because my baby needed his immunization shots. While I sat in the examination room, the doctor came in and said, "Jeanne, I enjoyed reading your books." And then he said, "I don't really know you that well, but are you a doctor?" And I said, "No." "Oh then, are you a nurse?" he asked. "No," I replied. "Did you always want to write books?" he asked. "No," again I replied. Perplexed he said, "Well, where did you get all of your information?" I answered, "*I am a mother*." And even he laughed and conceded that was indeed the superior answer.

22

Try to use a pediatrician who is a parent. You'll tend to get more sympathy, real-world advice and understanding—just what you need right now.

Well-baby checkups are done at:
2 weeks, 1 month, 2 months, 4 months,
6 months, 9 months, 12 months, 15 months,
18 months, and 24 months, and at each birthday that follows until your doctor says you are excused.

$\mathcal{I}$n the first few weeks postpartum, be sure to have a strong pain-relief medicine on hand for *you* when your uterus starts to contract to its prepregnancy size, and make sure your doctor approves it if you're breast-feeding. Some physicians will prescribe a pain reliever with codeine or something else to relieve the pain, and I can tell you, the feeling can be tremendous and it comes on unexpectedly. Ask for at least one or two samples from your doctor before you leave the hospital to have it on hand.

(p.s. I hope you got this book early enough to know this tip. Otherwise, ooh, ouch!)

Before calling your doctor's office with a concern about your baby, be sure you know your baby's temperature. Your doctor will ask about this right away.

It's unfortunate, but babies and young children for that matter, usually get sick with colds and fevers in the middle of the night. This is another reason for you to make sure you get enough rest.

Attempt to schedule your baby's doctor's appointment as the first one of the day or the first one back from the lunch hour so you won't have to wait in line. To save time, call a half hour before your appointment to see if the doctor is running on schedule.

Adjust your water heater to a maximum of 120° F or 49° C. This way, you will not accidentally scald your baby with the bath or tap water, and you will also save a great deal of money... Yay!

Every home with a baby should have two infant bulb syringes...one for noses and one for ears. They are made differently and have different uses. The nose syringe is especially helpful because you can clear a baby's stuffy nose with it just before feeding. He'll drink better, especially when he is sick.

Don't use a pillow, puffy comforter, or lamb's wool mattress cover in your baby's crib until she is old enough to lift her head and hold it up. Studies prove that these items contribute to Sudden Infant Death Syndrome (SIDS). Also, try putting your baby down to sleep on her back. If your baby objects, discuss it with your doctor.

$\mathcal{B}$abies like to be bounced gently, not shaken or patted too hard. Shaking or patting a baby too hard can severely injure him—or worse.

$\mathcal{B}$e careful not to move baby too fast in a stroller because she can't breathe against the flowing air, and be sure to turn your stroller seat around toward you when walking fast or exercising with baby. Be especially careful if you are an avid jogger and the baby is on your back, because you can't see how he is affected by your motion and movement. It's known that shaking an infant's brain causes serious problems.

If you are trying to give your baby medicine, use a nipple! Babies will suck the medicine from a nipple as though it were breast milk or formula, without knowing the difference.

Vitamins with iron can cause constipation in both you and your baby. Use a stool softener yourself and be aware of your baby's bowel-movement schedule for irritability. Never force anything up your baby's rectum to get him to go, no matter how desperate you get, because the baby will learn to depend on this unhealthy strategy. Just hold his legs up, bent at the knees, and apply pressure to the knees to help push out a bowel movement.

Don't overfeed the baby when he's constipated—that's the worse thing you can do. Less food may actually help him feel better and get him finally to have a bowel movement, especially as his body starts getting used to iron.

If your baby throws up regularly while in the car, it may not be car sickness. Make sure the car seat is in place properly and does not vibrate when the car is moving. It's actually the motion and vibrations that may be causing the baby to be sick. This can be true when jogging with baby, too.

Signs of ear infection include: playing with ears, loud/piercing crying, and high fever. Quick fact: ear problems in babies are frequently caused when fluid builds up in the ear and it becomes infected.

One of the major signs of dehydration is brick-colored urine—almost red looking. Make sure baby is urinating regularly and that his diaper is wet throughout the day. If not, increase feeding, add water, and call your doctor.

$\mathcal{F}$iling baby's nails is easier than cutting them, especially if your personal style is more like a bull in a china shop than like a ballerina.

$\mathcal{A}$s a general rule, new babies should never have bad breath. If your newborn does have bad breath, take her to a pediatrician immediately. It could be a sign of infection in the mouth or somewhere else in the body. The most common infection to cause this is called a thrush infection. It's easily treated when caught early and it happens in about 5 percent of babies. And, you know how I know this—right?

$\mathcal{B}$owel movements take on the color of mustard if baby drinks breast milk and becomes dark brown if he's on formula.

$\mathcal{W}$arm those cold diaper wipes in your hand before you change your baby. Also, use a diaper wipe, not just wet toilet paper or a paper towel (except when you're stuck somewhere without wipes). The people who say you can save money by not using a wipe when changing a diaper are forgetting the additional cost of the doctor visit when the baby gets a rash or fungus. Been there, seen that, done that.

The main difference between disposable and cloth diapers is the cost and the work for new moms and dads. Disposable diapers also generally cause a lot less diaper rash because the wetness is removed so well. It's the urine and wetness that cause diaper rash.

It's common for a blistering rash in the diaper area to be the result of a reaction to medicine. It's not treated the same way as traditional diaper rash and those methods—remedies like zinc oxide—probably won't work. In this case, it may require changing the medicine altogether. If your newborn has been prescribed any medicine, call your doctor so that it can be adjusted or changed.

Zinc oxide is a diaper-rash treatment and its purpose is to promote healing. To that end, check the warning label, but don't be surprised if it also recommends use on cuts and burns—so, don't forget to think of yourself now and then!

Air your baby daily. The best way to handle diaper rash is for your baby not to get it. Five minutes a day without a diaper really helps! Longs baths are good for relieving it, too.

Zinc oxide or petroleum jelly is used on diaper rash. These products create a barrier to protect the baby's skin from his diaper and bowel movements. They also soothe the skin and promote healing. If your baby has a diaper rash and diarrhea, be sure to use a barrier cream.

If you distinctly smell burning rubber in your house, check to see if a nipple dropped onto the heating element in your dishwasher.

It's hard to know, understand, or predict your baby's personality, mood, and overall composure at first. If you see your baby acting unusual—not sleeping regularly or at all, tense, alarmed, stressed, "bug-eyed," or anything else—this could be a symptom of a medical reaction. In the old days, babies didn't need or get any medicine, but medication is prescribed for both mom and baby sometimes now. Look out for this because your baby may be having a reaction to her own medicine...or to yours, especially if you're breast-feeding.

$\mathcal{U}$se sunscreen always, and especially between the hours of noon and 3:00 p.m. Keep sunscreen and a hat in your diaper bag because you'll need it when you least expect it. Babies with thin hair need this even more, and don't forget, nature made it easy to avoid the sun by taking naps during the 12–3 hours with infants.

$\mathcal{S}$exuality is part of life for all living creatures, so don't be surprised if you see your infant son with an erection or your infant daughter with secretions. This is normal and in fact, erections can be painful for young boys, so keep it in mind if they are crying uncontrollably.

If your baby all of a sudden cries out in pain with a red face, perhaps she has a lot of gas. Notice if you've changed something in her diet. For example, did you switch from breast milk to formula or from one formula to another recently? Whenever you change anything for a newborn—especially diet and medications—watch out for the reactions within 24–48 hours. If you think it's medication related, call the doctor. If you think it's food related, call the doctor anyway, but you can also either stay with the new mixture for at least another 48 hours—as long as there is no fever and the baby is drinking—or revert to the previous plan. Don't try a new plan or mixture because you have to eliminate the problem by finding out what it is first. You can't do this if you keep changing your plan or mixture. Monitor each mixture (e.g., the new formula) one at a time.

Babies wiggle! And for that reason, a baby will fall off any counter she is on. Always put babies safely on the floor, no matter what kind of carrying device or seat they are secured in.

***

Having a temperature means baby's body is signaling you that it's fighting off something. If your baby's temperature runs high, she may need help from the doctor. That's why keeping a thermometer (or four or five thermometers) on hand is so important.

Both babies and moms can have backlash at first, like gas from red peppers, onions, cabbage, etc. But don't forget you could have the same reaction from a simple piece of plain toast with butter, a bagel, or a vitamin. More often, it is true with rye or wheat toast, with some special or even generic spice, or flavoring as simple as garlic. Thank goodness, it does usually wear off shortly after everyone adjusts to the new foods.

Good old water is the best remedy for anything and everything...sick babies, tiredness, carpet spills, etc. Remember, some medications can just make it worse.

$\mathcal{I}$f you don't want anyone to touch your baby, that's okay. If you can't seem to say so directly, just say that the baby isn't feeling well and you don't want to risk spreading a virus to them and leave it at that. However, you should know that baby's immune system builds up by the number of infections they are around...not the opposite.

$\mathcal{I}$f your baby is sick, be sure to wash your hands and sterilize everything from your breast pump, the nipples, and bottles to your countertops and doorknobs. All of these actions will speed your baby's recovery.

It's hard to think out of the box when you're in a bind with a new baby, but it's vital to seek the obvious. Most problems with babies can be resolved with water, food, sleep, air, sunlight, smiles, diversion of attention, exercise, rocking, love, and a vaporizer with Vicks Vaporub. Wow—and they're all pretty much *free!*

Videotape your baby when she's doing something you don't think is normal and bring it to your doctor's office. Babies never seem to do what you want them to do when you want them to do it, so this is a perfect solution!

Chapter Four

Eating and Feeding

The most important element to peaceful breast-feeding or bottle-feeding, in order to be like those people in advertisements, is that *you* have to be the most peaceful of all.

Be patient. It takes time to develop a routine with your baby, especially your newborn, but patterns are everything and the earlier you start with your baby, the better. A routine is what your baby needs. You have to do it, do it again, do it again until she catches on, and always remember, it's far easier to repeat yourself now and in the early stages than to break any bad habits later.

Include dad in baby's feeding as early as possible—regardless of bottle or breast. Meaning, use a bottle with breast milk from the beginning if nothing other than to keep dad completely in the loop.

Babies give clues when they're hungry—
watch for them and save yourself from a
breakdown and/or public outburst. Signs
include gnawing on their hands, looking at you
for attention, and becoming anxious. Watch for
these signs and other body language clues and
you'll know it's time to feed.

The most important point about feeding is to
keep the nipple and baby's suction clear. It
doesn't matter if it's bottle-feeding or
breast-feeding. Once your baby is latched on
and relaxed, you'll be good to go using either
method.

ℬe efficient. Sterilize enough bottles and nipples and prepare enough feedings to last forty-eight hours instead of twenty-hour. Presto—you've just eliminated half of the work for yourself!

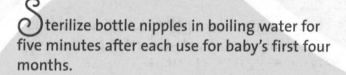

𝒮terilize bottle nipples in boiling water for five minutes after each use for baby's first four months.

$\mathcal{K}$eep the components of a bottle together in one place. Use all of the components each time you prepare a bottle. The cap prevents infection and is just as important as the nipple. It sounds so basic, right? It's just these are the types of things that you usually learn the hard way as a new parent because the baby will get an infection at the end of the day if you don't heed the warnings. Blah, blah, blah, I know you get it.

$\mathcal{H}$eads up! As store-bought nipples become sticky, replace them. Worn-out nipples keep the baby from drinking smoothly, which will bother him. It's also a good idea to leave new nipples with your baby-sitter, who may not recognize your baby's frustration with worn-out ones.

Read the directions for mixing formula with water and never deviate from the recipe. Some people try to dilute the formula to get their babies to lose weight. I've heard of others who try to make it stronger to fill up the baby so he'll sleep. All of these ideas are invalid and very unhealthy for your baby. The measurements for preparing formula should be done exactly as explained on the label. That's why it's called *formula*.

Use bibs. Babies spit up unexpectedly and it always ruins their nice new outfits, especially formula-fed babies because formula stains everything.

Consider that baby probably feels a whole lot better after she spits up than she did before. It may be a good time to give her body a rest from food or drink for a short period of time.

Burp your baby after every three ounces of liquid. If the baby doesn't burp by the time you count to three hundred, lay him flat on his back for sixty seconds. Then pick him up and resume burping him while you are standing...he'll burp then!

Generally speaking, it takes twenty minutes or so to feed your newborn baby, excluding burping, and the burping part is as important as the feeding part for new babies. This is true until they can burp naturally without any patting necessary. You'll know when that day comes because your baby will be sturdy and his burping will come on its own. And then in a few years, you'll have to teach him how to *stop* looking so natural at it in public...but that's down the line, so relax, and enjoy the moment of feeding your baby for now.

$\mathcal{L}$et your baby eat until she stops. As a rule, try to feed your newborn at least three ounces at a time. If she does not drink enough, she will be hungry continuously. If she does drink enough, she will sleep better at night.

$\mathcal{R}$otate your baby from left to right when you're feeding because she'll get cramps. Not to mention the cramps you'll get too if you stay too long on one side. Even if you're bottle-feeding, it's a good idea to rotate the baby from side to side—it's good for his eyesight too!

$\mathcal{A}$lthough sometimes it seems to take an eternity for a newborn to finish feeding, believe me, *the slower, the better!* Infants who drink too fast suffer from gas. Remember, gulp = gas.

$\mathcal{K}$eep calm when feeding your baby, especially while out dining. Be sure to choose a private spot with your back turned away from the public and just relax.

When feeding your baby before naps or bedtime, try giving her a portion of what she normally drinks. Then stop, change, and burp her (even if it means waking her up). After that, finish the feeding. This way, she won't fall asleep before she is finished eating and she will be more likely to enjoy a longer rest.

Good news...when baby is eating, he's exercising. So he's wearing himself out for a good nap! Take your time because it pays off later—or even better, immediately afterwards.

Some babies can seem frustrated just because they want to suck, not necessarily because they are hungry. You can feed her or you can simply knuckle/bend your clean finger and put it in her mouth to pacify her. If you always relieve the sucking urge with a breast or bottle, you're never going to be able to get anything done. The same thing goes for pacifiers. It's up to you, but remember babies become dependent upon just about anything given to them routinely.

Notice if your newborn baby is starving right after a bowel movement. This will help you identify her schedule and plan. Don't forget, write it down. It's easier to see in writing.

*I*s your baby suddenly hungry all the time? If you are considering feeding your baby oatmeal or rice early, keep in mind that growth spurts don't last very long. Give this stage a week or two and call your doctor before you make any decisions.

*T*he same is true for the reverse of the growth spurt. When baby seems to eat less than usual, this is normal. And of course, sometimes she is just not hungry. (I really wish I were like that.)

$\mathcal{I}$f your doctor says to feed your baby once every two hours, she means two hours from the beginning of the feeding, not the end. For example, if your baby eats his first meal at 7:00 a.m., then you should try feeding him again at 9:00 a.m. and then again at 11:00 am. And to make your life simpler, try to stick with feedings on the hour.

$\mathcal{W}$arm bottles are wonderful. They go down easy and they put babies right to sleep. But do give a room-temperature or even a cold bottle to your baby every now and then. He will find it strange, but it will prevent a major problem if you are caught unprepared later, when you can't make the bottle "just right" for some reason.

Once you give your baby juice, you can kiss those easy, sleep-inducing bottles of warm breast milk or formula goodbye. Babies usually prefer juice once they have tried it.

If you know you will be converting entirely from nursing to bottle-feeding on a certain date, watch for how your baby adapts to change in general. This will give you a better sense of how to introduce the bottle—slowly or rapidly. Babies have their own personalities and patterns. Some are needy and some will surprise you by not caring at all about anything. Notice this about your baby and I bet you the only "nipple confusion" you will experience will be which one to buy.

Chapter Five

Sleeping

Sleeping is the key to a peaceful baby and, just as important, it's the key to a peaceful home. Figuring out how to get a baby to sleep and get enough sleep may be a bit of a challenge, but think of it as a puzzle with each little piece having a purpose. Try to look at the big picture, rather than the small piece. For example, your baby may not sleep through the night for months, but if you focus on getting him to sleep longer and longer each night, even in small increments, you won't be as frustrated and he will begin to "get it."

Three of the most common misconceptions new parents have about sleeping through the night is that (1) they believe their baby is different from the other millions of babies born each year and throughout time, (2) they believe that their baby simply doesn't need that much sleep, and (3) they believe their new baby can climb out of the crib.

If you refuse to believe any of these ridiculous things, you are well on your way to developing successful sleeping patterns early with your newborn.

*R*emember, *all* babies need and *require* sleep, and most importantly, the more, the better.

*T*ry to get your baby used to sleeping anywhere from an early age. Don't always use the crib or bassinet for his naps. For example, from day one, let him take every other afternoon nap in a play yard or in a busy room, such as the family room, with some background noises, even the television.

Strive to put your newborn baby into the crib instead of the bassinet by six weeks of age. You don't want him to become too used to the bassinet. By eight weeks, your baby will be ahead of the game for sleeping through the night—and he will love having his own place.

Every now and then, put your baby into the crib before she falls asleep. This will teach her that it's okay to go to bed awake and alone.

$\mathcal{I}$'ve heard that babies who drink smoothly and take long, even swallows that you can see in their jawline are likely to sleep through the night earlier.

$\mathcal{L}$ove, softness, and calmness during bedtime feeding will relax baby faster.

I think babies can see in the dark and are comfortable in the dark because they're used to it from the womb. Experiment when trying to get your baby to sleep and notice if making her room pitch dark actually *helps* at all. If it doesn't, then try using a night-light over a lamp.

*D*on't turn on lights during night feedings. It may wake your baby.

Check baby at bedtime. Roll back his sleeves if they might cover his hands in the night. This way, he won't wake up later because he cannot get to his thumb or hand to soothe himself.

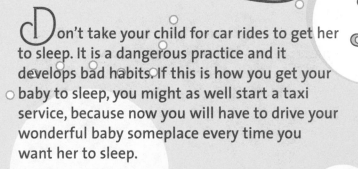

Don't take your child for car rides to get her to sleep. It is a dangerous practice and it develops bad habits. If this is how you get your baby to sleep, you might as well start a taxi service, because now you will have to drive your wonderful baby someplace every time you want her to sleep.

Sleep when your baby sleeps.

Try not to wake your baby to change a diaper unless she has had a big, runny bowel movement and really needs it. Good diapers are designed to handle these situations and last for hours.

$\mathcal{P}$ut your baby to bed in pants that are easy to change, in case an unexpected runny bowel movement comes along. This way, you can minimize her sleep disruption—and yours!

 $\mathcal{I}$f your baby wakes up in the night screaming, but does not open her eyes, as though she were still asleep, she may have a gas bubble. Try burping her or using a gas-relief product first. Don't immediately try to feed her; it could make her more miserable. And it may reverse all the progress you made in weaning her from night feedings.

If your baby falls asleep in the car, take her out of the car seat as soon as you get home and put her into her own bed. This simple practice will remind baby that she can go back to sleep after being moved. After all, she did it in the womb!

If your infant cries every time you put him down, try warming a thin blanket in the dryer first and then put him down on it. He will probably love it and quiet down immediately.

Let your newborn baby sleep! It depends on the baby of course, but more likely than not, your baby can sleep all day at this age and then sleep just as well at night. Check on him regularly, and I say, if he's okay, you're okay.

New babies often sleep when there are noises going on around them, especially sounds they do not recognize. It's almost like they're hiding from them. When it's absolutely quiet and your baby thinks the coast is clear, don't be surprised if she opens her eyes and even starts to coo. And if ever she coos, let her coo. And then tape- and video-record her as long as you can. Those moments are truly precious.

Sleep is not the only thing that relieves sleep deprivation for new moms and dads. Resting with your feet up and eating well will also do the job.

⁓

Getting a baby to sleep through the night is like testing the deep end of a pool. Prepare yourself mentally and venture a little further each night. Good news—eventually you will make it.

Try this. Each night, from now until the baby catches on, plan to put him to bed for the night at around 11:00 p.m.—not 7:00 p.m. Give him a bath at 10:30 p.m., play together a little, and then, after he's been stimulated and fed, put him down to sleep for good. Your goal should be to train baby to sleep the 12:00 a.m. to 5:00 a.m. shift first.

Ingredients for a good night's sleep: keep a routine for yourself and for the baby so that it's predictable, wear the baby out by stimulation or by having the baby naked just for awhile, and feed him well before bedtime.

As your baby grows, it gets harder to hear him cry, not easier; so if you're going to let your baby cry for intervals to get him to sleep through the night, do it between months two, three, and four and you'll be better off.

Once your baby weighs around thirteen pounds, you should be able to enjoy ten to twelve hours of uninterrupted sleep if he's eating enough during the day. The thirteen-pound mark is significant and it's usually a positive life-changing time for brand new parents. Hooray!

It's nice to have special moments when you're with your baby—rocking, hugging, kissing, reading, or singing lullabies, but if you do it every time, you'll set up a pattern and baby will only relax when you do it, so save these moments for lunch and morning and when you really need them otherwise. Spend the other times you have with your partner just relaxing. And if you can really do this, *you rock!*

The Golden Rule of sleeping through the night is this: if you turn on the TV or entertain your baby late at night even once, your baby will expect you to entertain her every night at that same time.

ou can fool Mother Nature once in awhile! Sucking is instinctive so if your baby ate at 11:00 p.m. and you put her to bed, try feeding her again at 1:00 a.m....even if she is sleeping. If she eats now, *you* may catch some uninterrupted sleep and avoid another middle of the night feeding.

 our baby will perform random "mom checks." If he checks for you in the middle of the night, let him know you are near by patting his back, but avoid picking him up. If you pick him up, he will remember his great success and try it again every night thereafter. Think, "bad habit, bad habit" whenever these moments come along.

Believe it or not, one of the main reasons that babies and their parents don't sleep well at night is that they are overtired. How bizarre is that? Keep yourself and your baby from being overtired by taking regular naps. Your baby will sleep better at night.

Exercising your baby for fifteen minutes or so before bed should help relax her unless she is overstressed. If so, perhaps soft music will work better.

By three months, your baby should be able to physically handle not eating during the night. However, she is used to being fed on demand, so first you have to concentrate on dropping the feeding, not on sleeping through the night. The way to do this is not only to stop the night feedings completely, but also change the way you feed her during the day. Don't jump up to feed her the moment she cries. She'll expect the same at night. Soon she'll adjust to the routine of not eating at night. It takes a good week to learn, although some would call it a "bad week."

Don't worry, all babies make liars out of their parents, especially when it comes to things like if you tell your baby-sitter she won't wake up while you're gone, because she will. Get used to it, they've got radar.

Chapter Six

Crying

Crying is an art form.

However, it can be stressful and aggravating at times, and it can raise a parent's blood pressure and freak them out completely—especially a new parent. It's how you look at it. It can actually be a lifeline between a parent and a child. How beautiful, right? Something that draws you closer together because it says, "I need you."

When your baby is crying, he is trying to reach out to you. I can tell you that I've noticed that when I am trying to get my baby to stop crying by rocking him on my shoulder, if my neck is tightened up, he gets even more upset. I believe he can tell that I'm tense and he's counting on me to help him. Whenever that happens, I take deep breaths, leave, take a bath—*whatever* to get back to realizing that it's not the baby that's cranky at that point—it's me! (Again...)

From the very beginning, babies learn to cry in different tones when they want different things. Watch for these distinguishing cries and you will learn what they need. Most important, you will also be able to tell the difference between their normal needs and when they are in pain.

Try not to make abrupt moves around your infant. Startled babies create crying frenzies.

Don't jump to conclusions and assume your baby has a colic condition just because she cries a lot. (Not that it matters, but you will sound ridiculous to other parents.) In fact, only about 20 percent of infants develop colic-like symptoms. A colicky baby by definition is one who cries uncontrollably for three hours or more, at least three days a week.

Colic is not considered a serious condition. It's unknown exactly what causes colic, but the most common factors are gas, a distressful situation at home, or it's just their disposition. The great news is that it usually doesn't start for a few weeks after the baby is born and it goes away in a couple of months on its own. The bad news is that it's really, really terrible for the new parents.

Generally speaking, medicine isn't used for treating colic either. Instead it's *motion* to relieve the tension and the gas. Things like taking a walk, using a swing, etc., can work wonders.

Babies cry when they are hungry, wet, bored, sick, tired, and just to relieve stress...so do postpartum moms!

Babies cry just as hard when they are tired and want to go to bed as they do when they are hungry and want to eat.

Try not to run to the rescue every time your baby becomes frustrated or cries. Let her first try to work out her problems for herself as long as she's not in need of something vital, like food. Your restraint, difficult though it may be, is going to teach baby a lifelong lesson of relying on herself sometimes. And you may not be thanking me for this tip now, but you will be thanking me later.

Regular periods of crankiness are baby's way of burning off stress, so be grateful for them! They usually only last until baby is as used to the real world as he was to the womb.

$\mathcal{S}$ome say some crying is actually good for babies because it helps develop their lungs. You'll begin instinctively to know when that kind of crying is okay, versus when it's not as you get used to being a parent.

$\mathcal{R}$emember, all babies are good; some just cry more than others.

$\mathcal{I}$f baby is crying uncontrollably and you think it may be gas, try lying him across your legs and rub or gently pat his back to release the gas. Just don't shake him.

$\mathcal{N}$ot sure why baby is crying? Well, keep in mind that babies don't like overstimulation, boredom, changes in their routines, loud and abrupt noises, and tense parents.

If the baby always cries with you and yet seems to relax with everyone else, don't get frustrated. Just give it time. You will eventually adapt to each other's personalities. After all, you are both learning about each other.

If you get overloaded yourself and can't stop the baby from crying, just put him down in his crib or bassinet and take a break. You could be making things worse and he may just want to be alone. Some babies truly like to be alone even if it's just for a few minutes per day.

To minimize crying, try a walk and change of scenery, but be completely quiet or just whisper until she gets composed. Your talking could be irritating her more—especially if she's overtired. Remember, while you were pregnant, you didn't have a lot of the hormones and challenges baby is enduring with you now. Try to act like you were when you were pregnant when around your baby...calm, happy, confident. And when you do this routinely, *wow*, what a difference you'll find in your baby.

After a baby has been crying uncontrollably for awhile, she may have forgotten why she is crying. Try rocking, dancing, or singing. And stay calm!

*R*unning water and fans can be peaceful to many babies—*or* one or both of those things can highly irritate them. You need to watch your baby to see what she likes and then use it all the time.

*I*f you get desperate because baby won't stop crying, take all of his clothes off and snuggle him warmly in a light draping blanket and then lay him down in a bassinet or crib under your careful eye. If nothing else, this will distract him and he'll probably fall asleep, perhaps just from the crying. Sometimes you've just gotta do what you gotta do.

$\mathcal{I}$f baby is crying, go through the checklist of other tips, but don't discount the one on boredom. Babies cry when they just want your attention.

$\mathcal{B}$abies remind me of rainbows because they usually show up shining brilliantly after a storm. And I've learned that for babies, "storms" can mean either crying or a bowel movement.

Chapter Seven

Must-Haves
and Must-Knows

I'm going to keep this part simple and just tell you what you absolutely need to have and know. And that should wrap it all up for you.

Don't hesitate to buy low-cost alternatives for some baby items, especially medicines. Often they are made by the same manufacturer and are exactly the same product as the higher-priced, advertised brand. Yippy!

House essentials: monitor(s), baby sling, crib, stroller, car seat(s), high chair(s), activity center, play yard, thermometers, nail clippers, diaper supply, changing table and pad, diaper pail, cotton balls, and at least one fan!

Buy formula, diapers, and wipes by the case. Your child will use these products for several more months with the exception of the smallest size, newborn diapers. Infants grow *so* fast that it's likely you will only require a few weeks supply of that size.

Diaper patterns are cut close but they are not the same, so take time if you're frustrated with the fit on your baby and use another diaper brand. The same is true for diaper rash. Some brands may cause your baby to get a rash, when others won't.

Let your baby finish his bowel movement before you change his diaper. Unless he has diarrhea, giving him a few minutes will save you a lot of diapers and a lot of diaper changing.

Did you know you can usually exchange unused diapers that are too small and baby food and formula that is unopened? Just take them back to the store where you bought them and usually, there are no questions asked if the expiration date, etc., are okay and the condition is acceptable.

The new bras and support garments on the market are incredible! Take all of the advice you can get from past moms on parenting, but look for the new generation of product offerings, which will make your life so much easier! Search for award-winning products, too. They've already done the testing for you. One less thing to think about!

Invest your next couple of extra dollars into the greatest invention ever made for parents—a remote-controlled car-starting device. With this gadget, you can start your car from inside the house and warm it up on cold mornings while you're still packing up the baby.

Diaper bag essentials: a hat, blanket, back-up nipple, pacifier, bottle, formula, baby powder, diapers and wipes, sunscreen SPF 15 or higher, back-up set of clothing, pain reliever, thermometer.

Be sure to get a play yard early and try putting your baby into a carrier seat and then place the seat inside her play yard for a few minutes now and then. She will get used to it this way. By the time she is ready for it, she will love spending lots of time there in her own special place that she's admired for so long. Cribs are the same way with babies—the more you get them used to it early, the more they learn to *love* it. And as a parent, the more you'll learn to *love* those places they love.

The other diaper bag *must-have* is a room deodorizer spray. It's imperative for when you're traveling on a plane or in a bus or train and baby goes #2. It's a lifesaver, not only for you and the baby, but for the other people around you. As a matter of fact, get two or three of these.

Other good ideas for travel once you get situated and the baby's a few months old are: age-appropriate toys and a play yard. Buy diapers when you get wherever you're going to avoid so much packing and lugging. Carry with you only the number of diapers you usually need plus an extra five and then gauge yourself.

$\mathcal{I}$f your monitor is battery-powered, you don't have to plug it in, so bring it with you everywhere you go.

$\mathcal{M}$ake sure you are listening to your infant. Sometimes your baby monitor may pick up other people's monitors and you'll hear their baby, especially if you live in a condo or town-house development. To test the monitor in the beginning, turn on a music box and then listen to the receiving end. If you hear the music, you'll know it's on the right channel and picking up your baby.

Also remember that other people's monitors may be picking up yours, so your best bet is to behave with your child as if someone else is listening.

Don't put a monitor next to baby's head or too close to your head. Put it elsewhere in the room. Don't keep the volume too high, because if you do, baby's frequent stirs and yawns are sure to keep you awake.

If you happen to end up with two or three baby monitors, don't return them immediately. Think: living room, master bedroom, kitchen, grandmother's house. Use them all! This way you avoid having to move them around the house.

If you have two sets of monitors and a large house, put the base of one and the receiver of the other upstairs. Then put the other receiver and base downstairs and turn both monitors on low. Ta dah! I've just installed an intercom system in your home. You're welcome.

Red Alert: If company is over and you meet in the baby's room for a private conversation with someone, don't forget to turn *off* the monitor. This is another one of those tips that you usually have to learn the hard way. Believe me, I know. Oops!

Most important, listen to your own internal "monitor" as it relates to baby's welfare.

Don't use heat fans unless you carefully monitor the temperature of the baby's room. Babies easily overheat and this could be extremely dangerous, especially if you close the baby's door.

$\mathcal{I}$n my opinion, fans are absolutely vital—especially as your baby grows into a toddler and beyond. That's why I'm spending so much time on this section. In short, train your baby early with a fan and it will save you years of sleeping issues.

$\mathcal{P}$lace a slow-moving fan in baby's room to circulate air. Turn it on each time you put your baby down to sleep. She will become conditioned to sleeping when she hears this noise. This is so handy when you're on vacation or visiting someone else's home. Babies can learn to sleep deeply with background noises.

$\mathscr{N}$ever point the fan or any air device directly at the baby.

$\mathscr{F}$ans drown out other noises, such as telephones, doorbells, televisions, dogs, fire engines, garbage trucks, sirens, and so on. Awesome!

$\mathscr{P}$lug the fan into an outlet that's operated by a wall switch because then you don't even have to enter the room if you want to turn it off or on. Turning off the fan may actually wake up the baby gently and naturally.

Ceiling fans are okay, but they can create drafts. That's why I recommend smaller or portable fans in the beginning, even clip-on ones are nice because you can point them in any direction you want. For example, place a fan towards the window or towards a closet, especially in the winter when there may be a draft in the room anyway.

Notice if a certain fan speed comforts or disrupts your baby. If it's on too high, it may irritate your baby, so try medium and low before you give up.

Babies love rattles. Rattles help them build dexterity with their hands. Make sure you give your baby a variety to experiment with.

In about the third month, baby is getting ready for an activity. Best type of toy: one that hangs just high enough above her that she can learn how to kick and swat at things. They are great for developing hand-eye coordination.

Keep your eye on the baby's mobile because they grow quickly and the distance between the mobile and baby gets closer and closer. Once an infant can reach it, it becomes dangerous. When you see the mobile getting close to the baby, drop your crib bed down another level.

Warning: Garage sales are fabulous for new parents, but you should never buy older items, especially juvenile furniture—like cribs and/or walkers and some toys, because the safety standards were so much different years ago. In fact, some items that you may remember as pleasurable may even have been recalled since then. Check the label for release date and for age appropriateness—and don't take any chances.

$\mathcal{I}$nvest in a baby jumper device. It will teach your baby how to belly laugh along with reminding you and your partner how to do so. Extra bonus: it also relieves gas! Let baby play softly by sitting upright and swinging without much movement in the 3–4 month area and then watch her go to town on her own after that. They are hilarious!

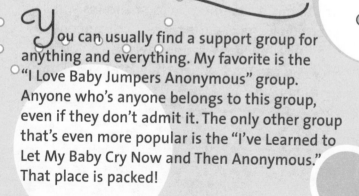

$\mathcal{Y}$ou can usually find a support group for anything and everything. My favorite is the "I Love Baby Jumpers Anonymous" group. Anyone who's anyone belongs to this group, even if they don't admit it. The only other group that's even more popular is the "I've Learned to Let My Baby Cry Now and Then Anonymous." That place is packed!

Leave tags on all the baby gifts you receive until you use them. Babies grow *so* fast. If you can't use some items, or even if you receive duplicates, you can return them for something else you do need if you don't take off the tag. And remember, some items you'll receive may make perfect gifts for someone else. Put a few generic ones away so if you get busy and can't get out to shop later, you'll have a gift on hand.

If friends or family give you an outfit, put it on your baby the next time they visit. They will know you appreciated it. If anyone ever asks you what size your baby is wearing, it's good to add on two sizes, because sizes vary and you can always use something that's too big, but you can't when it's too small.

I don't think sizes in children's clothing mean anything. For example, my son weighed fourteen pounds at three months, but my nephew weighed nine pounds. Which three-month-old did the tag refer to? Don't miss the joy of seeing your baby in a cute outfit because he outgrew it too fast. Try on everything early and learn to disregard the tags.

Don't overdress your baby just to visit a friend or go to the grocery store. How would you like it if you had to wear a business suit on your day off? Keep your baby comfortable and your life will be the same.

Observe your child for signs of individuality. For example, one of my boys liked to be completely undressed and was miserable unless his feet were free. The other one had to be completely bundled up at all times.

If your baby has cold hands, it could be a sign that he's underdressed. And remember, he may like it that way. Notice these things. They make a huge difference in baby's disposition.

Onesies are one-piece undershirts that snap under the bottom. They are fantastic because as your baby grows through the first year, you can put them on under his clothes and they will hold down his shirts and cover his tummy to keep him warm and snuggled.

$\mathcal{M}$ake a rule that you will only do laundry about once a week despite the temptation. Even though schedules are wonderful for you and the baby, you don't want to feel like you're on a treadmill that can't be adjusted to *your* needs.

$\mathcal{I}$f your baby's outfit is just a little too big, but you want him to wear it anyway, wash it first and throw it into the dryer to shrink it.

If an outfit is too big but has feet sewn into it, put it on your baby anyway. Then put a sock over each foot. If the outfit is too small, cut out the feet.

Babies grow so fast that you have to file their clothes to keep from going nuts. Keep the bottom dresser drawer empty and use it strictly for clothing that becomes too small. You will automatically start storing clothes together that are around the same size. You will also avoid having to hunt through all the drawers for something that fits. This goes on for a few years. When the drawer fills up, donate the clothes or put them away right then and there.

Take and store away one of your favorite infant outfits. Have it cleaned and then have it framed and put it away to be used as a shower or wedding gift for your child later in life. Other clothes that you want to save can be used for your baby's dolls. (Babies play with dolls regardless of sex a little later on.)

There are carriers on the market that will allow you to walk, shop, vacuum, and get things done without anyone knowing what you're doing including breast-feeding. If you're wondering how parents multitask, just get one of those!

Chapter Eight

Breast-Feeding

Breast-feeding protects your baby by supplying much-needed antibodies. Savor that thought and think of it as the beginning of a lifetime of protection that you are sacrificing for him...and if anything, try to do it in the first week when the colostrum—which is a fluid supplied with cells that defend the baby from infections—is delivered from you to your infant via your early breast milk. Be at peace knowing that you are looking out for your child.

It's been proven over and over again that breast milk adjusts to your growing baby, from colostrum to special fats that researchers are learning help build baby's cognitive development.

Be confident about nursing in public should you wish. It's your right!

Babies who are breast-fed can be easier to comfort than those who aren't.

Breast-feeding will assist your uterus in contracting to its normal size more quickly than if you aren't breast-feeding. And as many know, breast-feeding allows you to burn off more calories per day.

If you've adopted and want to breast-feed, try it! It's proven that mothers can breast-feed even without being pregnant or without delivering a child. It's because of breast stimulation. Why not give it a shot? Be patient because your body has to have time to respond to your request, but it does work. Be calm...be patient. A lactation consultant can help you.

Some babies are naturals at breast-feeding and some need to be taught. The same is true for mothers and motherhood.

Think of feeding baby as a natural, relaxing event. This is true if you're the parent and if you're breast-feeding or not. Be sure to take more time for yourself. Take a bath or let dad take the baby when you can and give yourself a break. Your being at peace drives the whole program.

Don't bother renting a breast pump because they are cheaper now than they used to be. Be sure to put one on your gift registry even if you're not sure you'll use it, since you can always return it.

Candidly speaking, I think every new mom has probably tried this when she's had a moment of privacy, but I used to go into the bathroom and kind-of pump my own breast milk into the sink. You can actually see if there is a blocked duct this way. After awhile, you might feel like a shower faucet, but I tell you, you'll never have any problems and neither will the baby when you can see what's going on.

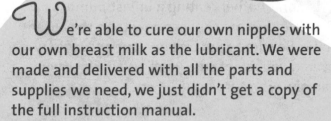

We're able to cure our own nipples with our own breast milk as the lubricant. We were made and delivered with all the parts and supplies we need, we just didn't get a copy of the full instruction manual.

There are at least three ways to nurse your baby comfortably, but which way you choose is completely up to you. Remember to use pillows to prop up the baby so it feels natural to you and so you can relax and let the milk flow rather than be tense and create a less relaxing experience for both you and the baby.

The three ways are:
(1) From the breast, the baby lies across the mother's stomach left or right.
(2) From the breast, the baby's legs are straddling the mother's leg—almost like a standing position. (This is great for tall mothers.)
(3) From the breast, the body of the baby goes around towards the mother's back...either side.

123

While nursing you have to have nutrients too, so you should eat the best you can while you're doing this. If you don't have a lot of milk to give the baby, try increasing the amount of water you drink during the day. Just walk around with a ten-ounce water bottle and drink it all the time. Relax and eat well!

Being discreet about nursing in public is the key because people fight over whether it's sexual or natural. Try not to lean on the sexual side or you'll backpedal on all of the work that the other moms have done and accomplished for all women. Wear easy-lifting shirts, a carrier, or whatever to keep it from being a controversial issue for you or anyone else.

$\mathcal{D}$o yourself a favor when in public and feed the baby at the first sign of hunger and before she gets out of control. You can even do it from your car before you enter a mall or anywhere else for that matter if you're worried about her schedule. Be sure to allow yourself enough time.

$\mathcal{Y}$ou shouldn't feed a baby breast milk that's been exposed to room temperature for more than eight hours according to the books. (I say six hours or they will throw up.) Also, you can only freeze breast milk once or it becomes dangerous for the baby.

If you're really tired, be careful when breast-feeding your baby, especially if you are lying down. Try to take a break first if you can—maybe a fifteen minute nap to refresh yourself. Or feed the baby a little, put her down in her bassinet or crib, and then take a short nap, so that you can care for your baby properly. Sometimes when you're tired, you don't make the best judgment calls, and you don't have the same coordination as when you feel refreshed, so train yourself to take a quick nap at times like this.

Breast milk needs to be frozen after it's been in the fridge for more than three days. You can't let it stay in the freezer for more than one year. But, hello—you don't want to give your baby freezer-dried breast milk at twelve months, do you? Just get rid of it every few weeks and if you can't, make a shrine in your backyard—even plant a small tree and water it. It's such an emotional time for you, but you have to keep things moving along in order to keep yourself sane. Later, when your kids grow, you'll be able to say, "This is my own breast milk area"…It may be better than keeping a scrapbook for you.

Sometimes when you wean too fast, your breasts become engorged and painful. Weaning slowly can avoid problems like this for you.

If you get a fever, be alert. It could be the sign of an oncoming breast infection.

$\mathcal{I}$f you have a clogged breast duct, try massaging it out—or better yet, let your baby suck it out. I'm pleased to introduce you to *remedy au naturale*. The common medical belief is that the women who get pregnant while breast-feeding do so because they don't nurse their babies *routinely*. In short, the body gets confused over this. The body begins the normal menstrual cycle again because it thinks mother stopped nursing, when she didn't. Wow, I just learned this!

$\mathscr{I}$f you have a breast infection, keep your breasts aired out as much as possible. It's like diaper rash. Air prevents the infection and air cures it. How simple, huh?

$\mathscr{D}$on't forget—the more you pump, the more milk you make, so if you're getting started and even if your baby is not latching on correctly, pump yourself and you will start to deliver a flow like a cow. As your baby grows, you'll start to see how everything is connected, and it's all so natural you kind-of have to laugh.

If you're about to break out of breast-feeding, drop the middle of the night feeding first since baby is tired and you'll have that to assist you. Dropping the morning feeding will be easier once you've dropped the middle of the night or evening feeding. You need to wean *slowly* for both of you.

Use your resources! La Leche League—so many others, and the Internet are your 24/7 support systems.

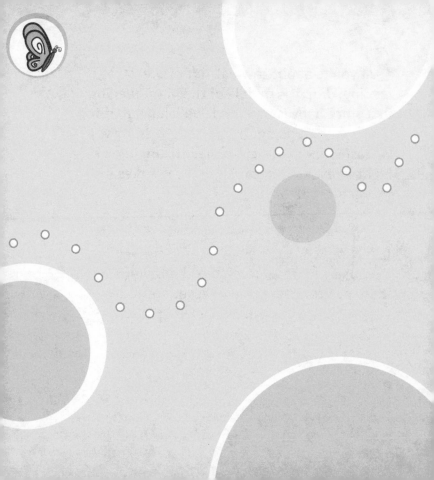

At this point I think you and I are up-to-date on parenthood and I'll think of us as friends from here on out. If you've read this much, you've got everything in my head at your fingertips, and if you'd like more, look for my other books of tips for parents.

Remember, God has given you a gift of being partners in creation and it's the *best* gift.

Lots of love & joy,
—Jeanne

Index

135